The New Face of Disabilities

Melica Niccole

The New Face of Disabilities

Hampton Publishing House, LLC

P.O. Box 29001

Columbus, OH 43229

Copyright © 2015 by Melica Hampton

Printed in the United States of America

Written by

Melica Niccole

Introduction by

Melica Niccole

Book Desiged by

Joshua Jadon

Edited by

Janet Slike

Publishing Company

Hampton Publishing House, LLC

Dedication

This book is dedicated to those who are trying to
make a difference in life, whether you are a person
who has a disability, a part of the support system,
or a service provider. Collectively, we can make a
difference.

I would like to thank the staff at Newark Public
Library in Newark, New Jersey. The reference team
at the library aided me in my research methods in
finding the employment information I needed when
I was at an impasse. Your efforts in helping to bring
this project together is appreciated.
Thank you!

Table of Contents

Introduction

Some people live in society without knowing the full extent of having a disability, yet they still make judgments about disabilities and the people who have them. It's getting tougher and tougher trying to visually assess who has a disability and who does not because the face of disability is changing. Take Viktoria Modesta, for example, who is "the world's first amputee pop artist" (WNBC Channel 4, 2014). She represents the opposite of what some people consider the characteristics of someone who has a disability.

She has overcome her disability and can do what some have perhaps told her that she could not do. In the information provided below, you will see that there are others like her, and you cannot always judge people by what is misunderstood or misrepresented. What would you do if you had the absolute capability of completing a job, yet you were overlooked because of your physical appearance? What do you do if you can't control your slurred speech and a warehouse interviewer chooses not to hire you? What if you lacked the social skills to interact with others, but your work was magnificent? These are some of the same things that people with disabilities are facing. They are willing and able to work but are often overlooked because of their disability. The number of individuals living with a disability is increasing

significantly, and it is becoming more and more

challenging to tell who has a disability. Some

people have a great fear of disclosing their

disability because of their concerns with being

treated unjustly for having it. Is treating people

different fair? There are many questions that you

should ask yourself when understanding people

with disabilities, including: What is a disability?

Who is at risk of developing a disability? What

should I do if one of my co-workers or a staff

member has a disability? Should I treat someone

with a disability differently than other people? All

of the questions above will be answered

throughout the text, which will give you a better

understanding of people living with a disability.

You Have a Right to Know

You have a right to know information regarding individuals with disabilities. Every day, we meet someone who has a disability whether it is mental, physical, or social. Your best friend or your favorite cousin could have a disability; however, he or she has found a creative way to cover it. What would you do if your daughter was born with a disability? Would you give her all the support that she needs? Or would you disown her and give her up for adoption? In some cultures, having a disability brings about feeling "helpless, depressed or blaming themselves or ancestors when they discover a disability in themselves or their family."   (Kim-Rupnow; Paragraph 3, 2001).

Do you think you would have the strength to place

her in an institution, like that of "Willowbrook"

(Unforgotten: Twenty-Five Years after

Willowbrook, 2014). These are questions that you

really need to ask yourself because nothing in life is

guaranteed and you want to be well prepared for

any circumstance. When putting things into

perspective, it would be great to know the type of

disability she has, the characteristics of individuals

with that type of disability, and the type of support

systems and services available. You should also

note that not everyone with the same disability

acts similarly. A person's home environment,

various learned skills, and other factors also play a

role in how an individual acts.

I am 100% sure that I would want to know everything that I could on the specific disability that my child was born with or had developed. It is only fair that my child be given an opportunity to develop within society and be able to cope with particular limitations and turn them into assets. I am not sure if most of you are familiar with the movie *Rain Man"* In the movie, Dustin Hoffman plays Ray, a man who has autism. His character was institutionalized as an adolescent (Levinson, B; 1988). If you are familiar with people who have autism, then you know that their disability deals with their social skills. His social skills were not able to develop to their fullest potential, probably because of his limited socialization with those outside of his living environment. I want you to imagine going out to eat and only being allowed to eat certain foods. You see other people eating the foods they want to, but you cannot. If you are anything like I am, you like to have options. Options allow you to experience different things and choose those things you like and reject those you do not. However, if you are familiar with those with autism, you will know that socializing with others is very hard for them.

Let's think about the difference you would have seen in Ray if he had been a part of society. He could have perhaps been a car salesman like his brother, a retail associate, or even a contestant on his favorite game show: *Jeopardy*. Sometimes, society knows not what it does, in the choices made that are intended to help people. The

13

decision almost always seems great at that particular moment but can be detrimental in the future. This is probably because a thorough review of the long-term effects on the individual or society has not taken place.

A while back, I was speaking with some previous acquaintances about working with people with disabilities. One of these acquaintances stated that she could not understand how I could work with people with disabilities. She then asked me, "Are you scared?" My first thought was "Of what? What in the world do I have to be afraid of?" Being honest with myself, I could understand where she was coming from. A few years ago, I thought the same way she did. I was applying for jobs so I could leave a long-term care center and came across a position working with individuals with disabilities. I did not apply for the position when I first saw it because I was a little nervous. What if someone had a panic attack or something happened that I had never been trained to deal with? I kept seeing the position in the newspaper week after week. I finally decided to apply for the position because after 3.5 years in my current position, I was ready for a career change. It was obvious that I was not the management material that my current job was looking for, so I decided to be another company's management material.

My expectations about the position changed immediately because I completed formal training before I was placed in a position with the organization. Matter of fact, I received certification from the Ohio Department of Developmental Disabilities, ongoing support from managers and other staff members, and a multitude of information and support from like organizations. It was amazing how so much information was bestowed upon me once I took the first step in working with this population. In thinking about my decision to leave my last job, I would not change the choice I made because working with people with disabilities has allowed me to progress so much within the field. I am very proactive in my individuals' lives and the trainings help me stay abreast of what I need to know.

Types of Disabilities

The Centers for Disease Control and Prevention (CDC) define developmental disabilities as a "group of conditions due to an impairment in physical, learning, language, or behavior areas. About one in six children in the U.S. have one or more developmental disabilities or other developmental delays." (Centers for Disease Control; Developmental Disabilities, 2013). These impairments include, but are not limited to autism, Down syndrome, traumatic brain injury, cerebral palsy, hearing loss, intellectual disability, visual impairments. These impairments deal with language, mobility, learning, self-help, and independent living.

A few years ago, The Ohio Department of Developmental Disabilities chose to take the "MR out of MRDD" (Taking the MR out of MRDD, 2008). In doing this, individuals with mental challenges were no longer considered as mentally retarded developmentally disabled. They would be considered as having a developmental disability. This was a great thing to do on their behalf, as individuals who were labeled as this were being unjustly scrutinized. In this day and time, some individuals with developmental and other disabilities are still being unfairly judged. The information below will assist you with working with individuals with disabilities, refraining from judging them unfairly, and explain things you should know about them.

Specific Learning Disability is a type of learning disability that is dependent on the person. People with Specific Learning Disability may need extra time with reading materials or taking tests, understanding the subject matter, completing math problems, or whatever objective is outlined in their Individual Education Plan (IEP). The standard definition "adopted by most (including U.S. legislation) is as follows: Specific Learning Disability means a disorder in one or more of the basic psychological processes involved in understanding or in using language, spoken or written, which may manifest itself in an imperfect ability to listen, think, speak, read, write, spell, or do mathematical calculations." (Learning RX; Specific Learning Disabilities, 2014).

Cognitive Disorders (CD) are "mental conditions that cause people to have difficulty thinking clearly and precisely. Symptoms are generally marked by impaired awareness, perception, reasoning, memory, and judgment." (Learning RX; Cognitive; Disorders, 2014)

Emotional/Behavioral Disorder (ED) is recognized as an "emotional, behavioral or a mental disorder. Students with such disorders are categorized as having an emotional disturbance." Some characteristics of this disorder are an "inability to learn that cannot be explained by intellectual, sensory, or health factors; an inability to build or maintain satisfactory interpersonal relationships with peers and teachers; and

inappropriate types of behavior or feelings under

normal circumstances."(Gallaudet University, 2014)

Autism, sometimes connected with

Asperger's, is "a group of developmental

disabilities that can cause significant social,

communication and behavioral challenges."

(Centers for Disease Control and Prevention;

Autism Spectrum Disorder, 2014)

MedlinePlus recognizes seizures as the

"physical findings or changes in behavior that occur

after an episode of abnormal electrical activity in

the brain. Some of the causes of seizures are

abnormal levels of sodium or glucose, brain

infection, brain injury, epilepsy, and stroke."

21

(National Institutes of Health; MedlinePlus,

Paragraph 1, 2014)

Down syndrome is "a condition in which a

person is born with an extra copy of chromosome

21. People with Down syndrome can have physical

problems, as well as intellectual disabilities. Every

person born with Down syndrome is different."

(National Institutes of Health; MedlinePlus,

Paragraph 1, 2014).

The Centers for Disease Control (CDC)

identifies cerebral palsy (CP) as a group of

disorders that affect a person's ability to move and

maintain balance and posture. CP is the most

common motor disability in childhood. CDC

estimates that an average 1 in 323 children in the

U.S. have CP." (Centers for Disease Control and Prevention, 2014).

Deaf or hearing loss is recognized as a condition in which individuals have no or deficient hearing and must mainly communicate through the use of American Sign Language (ASL) and/or lip reading. Individuals with this condition may benefit from hearing aids or cochlear implants.

Visually impaired "Vision loss can be caused by damage to the eye itself, by the eye being shaped incorrectly, or even by a problem in the brain. Babies can be born unable to see, and vision loss can occur anytime during a person's life." (Centers for Disease Control and Prevention, 2014)

According to the CDC, people "with ADHD may have trouble paying attention, controlling impulsive behaviors . . . or be overly active. Although ADHD can't be cured, it can be successfully managed, and some symptoms may improve as the child ages." (Centers for Disease Control and Prevention, 2014)

CDC recognizes fragile X syndrome (FXS) as the "most common known cause of inherited intellectual disability." Individuals with this syndrome may experience episodes similar to anxiety attacks and as if certain tasks or measures are unbearable. When working with of individuals with this syndrome, take your time, assist the individual with learning to pace themselves, write details out, obtain suggestions from their support systems, and try different methods to see what works. (Centers for Disease Control and Prevention, 2014)

Traumatic brain injury (TBI) "is defined as a blow or jolt to the head or a penetrating head injury that disrupts the function of the brain. A TBI can result in short or long-term problems with independent function." (Brain Injury Alliance New Jersey, Paragraph 4, 2014).

Intellectual disability (ID) "was previously called mental retardation. Individuals with ID have limits to their ability to learn at an expected level and function in daily life. ID can cause a child to learn and develop slower than other children of the same age" (Centers for Disease Control and Prevention, 2014).

The National Institutes of Health recognizes Tourette syndrome as "a neurological disorder characterized by repetitive, stereotyped, involuntary movements and vocalizations called tics" (National Institutes of Health, 2014).

Questions to Ask Yourself

Questions you may want to ask yourself when dealing with people with disabilities include: Who is at risk of developing a disability? What should I do if one of my co-workers or a staff member has a disability? And should I treat someone with a disability differently than other people?

Did you know that "About one in every 33 babies (3%) born in the U.S. are born with a birth defect. Birth defects are the leading cause of infant deaths and make up 20% of those deaths. Babies are at a greater risk of dying from a birth defect or having a long-term disability." (Centers of Disease

Control and Prevention, 2014). Some of these birth defects are things such as spina bifida, cardiovascular defects, cleft palate, and gastrointestinal issues. It is interesting to see how birth defects, including those caused by the mother's poor health or use of alcohol or drugs can cause long-term disabilities.

Thinking about disabilities and who is at risk of acquiring them can be very challenging to do. Take for example an individual who is deaf with two deaf parents. People may automatically assume that the deaf person's condition is hereditary. This is not necessarily true. It is a fact that a deaf couple can have children who can hear. If the disability is detected early, appropriate treatment can be applied, making the person's life easier and, in some cases, possibly preventing the condition from worsening. This means that individuals must pay attention to their children's speaking patterns, social skills, and other habits in order to seek the appropriate professional help needed.

If you work in an environment in which a co-worker has a disability or your customers have disabilities, you should try to use empathy in working with these individuals. This means that you should try to put yourself in the person's place when dealing with them. One thing I have noticed as a professional working with individuals with disabilities is that empathy is not always used when working with these individuals. Not to say that the person has chosen the opposite of using empathy, just perhaps that empathy had never been taught to them. This statement can be compared to managing finances and money. Some people can recognize that as children and adolescents they were never taught how to manage their money. This could be the very reason why they are in financial failure and have yet to manage their income and expenses effectively. I'm here to tell you that it's not too late for them and it's not too late for you to show empathy. Empathy can be shown by people putting themselves in the person's shoes, understanding how the person is feeling, and knowing whether or not the person understood the information explained to them. Another way empathy can be shown is by people lowering themselves down to the level of the other individual. An example of this is regarding a person in a wheelchair. When a fully mobile person explains information to a person in a wheelchair, it only seems fair that the person would sit down in a chair to talk to the person at eye level. This way the same amount of power is shared between the two, and the other person does not exert too much power over the individual by standing and making the person feel powerless.

When interacting with people with disabilities, people should treat them with the same respect and courtesy as others, no matter what the disability is... It goes without saying that everyone should be treated the same way and with some type of respect. Take for instance a visually impaired individual who had a hard time understanding an explanation. Does it make more sense to increase one's tone so the person can hear better or to paraphrase the statement, so the information is more readily received? Some people choose to increase their pitch thinking that the higher volume will somehow explain the original statement. In a situation like this, it's better to paraphrase the information or ask the individual to see what information her or she did not understand.

Steps in Working with Individuals with Disabilities

There are no specific steps that people have to follow in working with a person with a disability. Matter of fact, you may talk with many different people in the field and get a variety of answers. My objective in creating the steps below was to allow individuals to be proactive in working with this population.

Step 1- Don't Be Afraid of the Unknown.

The lack of reliable information can cause things or people to be misjudged or labeled to act in a particular way. Take my acquaintance for example. Sometime in her life, she was told or imagined that people with disabilities were scary individuals. This could not be further from the truth. The actual truth is that people with and without a disability can be equally intimidating. Just think about a neighbor who never says hi, but watches every move you make. Some people call this person "Nosey Rosey or Mr. Nosey." This person may or may not have a disability, but the action can be disturbing and unnerving to some people.

It is time to stop making judgments based on fictitious information, what someone else said, or what is viewed by a method of what I call "on the outside looking in." Now, you have immediate access to resources that can assist with your search for valid and reliable information on disabilities. The World Wide Web allows you to search for practically anything and everything. You, the researcher, have to make a judgment call, and the call is whether or not the information you are viewing is reliable. A good search might include reading information from organizations that work with people who have disabilities. Your search may take you to the Ohio Department of Developmental Disabilities, Opportunities for Ohioans with Disabilities, Bureau of Vocational Rehabilitation Services Commission, Franklin County Board of Developmental Disabilities, ARC, and Division of Vocational Rehabilitation. There are many other names you can search; however, this gets the ball rolling and allows you to search reliable systems.

While looking for valid and reliable information, remember people are sometimes afraid of the unknown. The unknown is new territory that has never been traveled, and some people like to get other people's opinions before making an important decision. Like Nike says, "Just do it." Make the commitment to learn something new. Who knows? You may appreciate your experience and encourage others to do the same thing.

Step 2- Treat Everyone the Same.

Managers, co-workers, friends, and family members should remember this statement, "Treat everyone the same." It is not encouraged that an individual or an employer provide preferential treatment to those with disabilities that is not available to other individuals or employees. Providing preferential treatment does not assist individuals with building skills and allowing them to function successfully within society. If needed, I do suggest that companies allow the individual to have a reasonable accommodation. A reasonable accommodation is a modification in the person's job, responsibilities, or tools which would assist them because they have a visual, physical, or another impairment,

As a positive behavior shaper, it is not only the duties of community agencies to help shape positive behaviors, but the community as well. The community plays a huge role in teaching and maintaining behaviors. It is our responsibility to provide these individuals with the right tools to be independent because they so want to live in autonomy. They want to do things on their own, shop on their own, pay bills, and live by their own will. One way you can help make individuals with disabilities more responsible is to hold them accountable for their actions or group's activities. This absolutely does not mean to yell at them or talk to them in an unprofessional manner. It means to help teach them the right way to do things.

I remember about a year or two ago, I was training this individual to prepare her for competitive employment. When she obtained competitive employment, her co-workers began helping her with her assigned work and doing

things for her that were not done for others. My

supervisor and I thought it was very important that

the staff allow the individual to complete the

duties on her own because we did not want her to

start expecting certain privileges from her co-

workers. There was another employee with the

company who thought the same thing and

expressed that she had previous experience

working with someone with a disability. The

employees finally allowed the individual to

complete the duties on her own and were amazed

by the transformation that had taken place. The

individual was very reserved from the start and had

shown coaching was needed in regard to her social

skills. In coaching the individual, I allowed her to

watch me complete the duties, asked questions, and provided feedback when needed. I also have to know the individual to build a relationship toward a successful outcome.

Step 3- Be Patient and Meet People Where They Are.

You should know that some things take time and as a well-known statement says, "Rome was not built in one day." When you are teaching someone a new skill or duty, you have to be patient with that person. You must allow them time to process the information and be able to deduce important information from what was taught. You should also note that not everyone learns the same way. Some people are verbal learners, while others are visual learners. As a previous job coach and job developer and a current work readiness instructor, I meet people where they are, whether it is socially, mentally, or physically. What this means is that I must understand people. I must understand their likes, dislikes, social activities, family structures, and other important information. I cannot expect people to know certain skills if those skills have never been taught. I also must focus on the positive attributes of the individual and things that they excel in doing.

One of my previous clients came from an impoverished neighborhood. She walked around with a demeanor that she was hardcore, and no one wanted to make mad. It was evident that she was taught this way of life to protect her from being hurt and taken advantage of from her environment. At first, it was not easy for me to break through her tough exterior because, to her, I was an intruder. I had nothing she wanted and could not relate to anything she was going through. Well, that was what she thought. Since I was also raised in an impoverished neighborhood, I had something she needed, the knowledge to push through all the tightly wrapped packages and reveal my true self. I let her in on my past and some of the things I had to deal with in having a "tough girl exterior." This conversation is what led her to open up more and allow me to meet her where she was and not to expect the impossible. This was a great breakthrough for me and allowed me to continue to mentor her and assist her as the position allowed me to do so.

Step 4- Know that the Disability Does Not Make the Person.

Too often, people are judged based on their disability and not the "content of their character' (King, Jr., 1963). Sometimes people may think that individuals who have disabilities are unable to complete certain tasks because of that disability. Say you are helping an individual who is visually impaired try to find work. Would you think that this individual should apply for a call center position? Some employers may believe that they will not be successful because the work environment is not conducive to their disability. In situations like this, the person who is visually impaired should contact his or her local disability center and get more information on assistive technology. Certain programs, such as JAWS and other screen reader devices can assist individuals with being successful in such positions. There are multitudes of other technologies a job candidate can recommend that can assist an organization with becoming disability accessible.

Another example I can offer up is of an individual who has Asperger's and/or autism. Sometimes, individuals with these disabilities will display signs of needing extra assistance when completing certain tasks that require them to socialize. In the past, I worked with this individual who had a cognitive disorder, autism, Asperger's, and ADHD. In this field, it is very common to see

individuals with a dual diagnosis (mental disability

and physical disability) or learning disability and

mental health issue. Prior to working with this

individual, others immediately prejudged him as

not being able to complete certain tasks because of

his disabilities. In working with this population,

just know that some things take time and having a

certain disability does not indicate that a person

cannot complete certain duties. It just makes your

job more interesting and challenging. Tell me this,

who does not like a good challenge in life? I for

one can state that I love a good challenge. I love

completing tasks that others are unable to

complete. When someone tells me that something

cannot be done, I laugh and say, "Well, maybe they

have not met me." In this situation, I am not being cocky about my skills and abilities. Please know that I will admit when I am unsuccessful in completing a task; however, I will try at least two to three times before that is done. I know that the disability does not make the person and that their training and support systems allow them to learn and move toward gaining more independence, whether it is related to work, home life, or social activities.

Step 5- Seek Specialized Help.

Getting specialized help means to acquire help from companies, organizations, and people that specialize in helping people with disabilities. These individuals are familiar with this population, know various services that could assist them, and would possibly be willing to come out and complete disability training sessions with your employees, friends, and acquaintances. These services include, but are not limited to, school programs, young adult and adult programs, work programs, and transition programs. Many of these programs teach skills such as: social, health and wellness, independent living, conflict resolution, financial and money management, and work skills. Some of the community resources include Centers for Disease Control, Ohio Department of Developmental Disabilities, Ohio Rehabilitation Services Commission (BVR), Franklin County Board of DD, Goodwill Columbus, and Catholic Social Services. In the next section, you will find

47

information on some of the community resources in Ohio, New Jersey, New York, Washington DC, Maryland, and Georgia. There are also a few federal agencies that are listed below to assist you with looking for resources on a wider scale.

Community Resources

World Health Organization (WHO)

<u>Mission</u>: "Seeks to publish and disseminate scientifically rigorous public health information of international significance that enables policymakers, researchers, and practitioners to be more effective. It aims to improve health, particularly among disadvantaged populations."

> <u>Address</u>: 525 Twenty-third Street, N.W., Washington, DC 20037
>
> <u>Telephone</u>: 202-974-3000
>
> <u>Website</u>: http://www.who.int/topics/disabilities/en/

National Institutes of Health (NIH)

Mission: "Seek fundamental knowledge about the nature and behavior of living systems and the application of the knowledge to enhance health, lengthen life, and reduce illness and disability."

Address: 9000 Rockville Pike, Bethesda, MD 20892

Website: http://www.nih.gov/

Centers for Disease Control and Prevention (CDC)

Mission: "Works 24/7 to protect America from health, safety, and security threats, both foreign and domestic. Whether diseases start at home or abroad, are

chronic or acute, curable or preventable,

human error or deliberate attack, the CDC

fights disease and supports communities

and citizens who do the same. The CDC

Increases the health security of our nation.

As the nation's health protection agency,

the CDC saves lives and protects people

from health threats. To accomplish its

mission, the CDC conducts critical science

and provides health information that

protects our nation against expensive and

dangerous health threats, and responds

when they arise."

Address: 1600 Clifton Road, Atlanta,

GA 30329-4027

Telephone: 800-CDC-INFO (1-800-232-4636)

Website:
http://www.cdc.gov/ncbddd/disabilityandhealth/types.html

Ohio Department of Developmental Disabilities (ODDD)

Mission: "To continually improve the quality of life for Ohio's citizens with developmental disabilities. To this end, the department has recently adopted a new person-centered philosophy. The approach is aimed at transforming service delivery to ensure that the person being served is at the center—and often a part of—all decision-making. By focusing on

personalized plans and outcomes, which

address what is important to and important

for the individual, programs allow

individuals to thrive and grow in society."

Address: 30 East Broad Street, 13th

Floor, Columbus, OH 43215

Telephone: 1-800-617-6733

Website:

http://dodd.ohio.gov/Pages/default.aspx

Opportunities for Ohioans with Disabilities

(OOD)

Mission: "To provide individuals with

disabilities opportunities to achieve quality

employment, independence, and disability
determination outcomes."

Address: 150 E. Campus View
Boulevard, Columbus, OH 43235

Telephone: 1-800-282-4536 or 614-
438-1200

Website: http://www.ood.ohio.gov/

**Franklin Country Board of Developmental
Disabilities (FCBDD)**

Mission: "To provide programs, services,
and support to eligible children, adults, and
their families so individuals with
developmental disabilities can live, work,
learn, and participate in the community."

Address: 2879 Johnstown Road,

Columbus, OH 43219

Telephone: 614-475-6440

Website: http://fcbdd.org/

Goodwill Columbus

Mission: "Building Independence, quality of

life, and work opportunities for individuals

with disabilities and other barriers."

Address: 1331 Edgehill Road,

Columbus, OH 43212

Telephone: 614-294-5181

Website:

http://www.goodwillcolumbus.org/

Catholic Social Services (Payee Services)

Mission: "Motivated by faith, reverence for life, and concern for the poor, Catholic Social Services advances the human dignity and potential of individuals and families by providing essential and compassionate social services and advocating for people in need."

Address: 197 E. Gay Street, Columbus, OH 43215 (main office)

Telephone: 614-221-5891 (main office) 1-800-536-5057 Ext. 1 (payee services)

Website: http://colscss.org/payee-services/

Commission on the Blind and Visually Impaired (Assistive Technology Services)

Mission: "Promotes and provides services in the areas of education, employment, independent living, and eye health through informed choice and partnership with persons who are blind or visually impaired, their families, and the community."

Address: 153 Halsey Street, 6th Floor, NJ 07101

Telephone: 973-648-7504

Website: http://www.nj.gov/humanservices/cbvi/home/

Division of Developmental Disabilities (DDD)

Mission: "Assures the opportunity for individuals with developmental disabilities to receive quality services and supports, participate meaningfully in their communities, and exercise their right to make choices."

Address: 195 Gateway Center, 5 Commerce Way, Suite 100, Hamilton, NJ 08691

Telephone: 1-800-832-9173

Website: http://nj.gov/humanservices/ddd/home/

Goodwill Industries of Greater New York and Northern New Jersey

Mission: "Goodwill Industries empowers individuals with disabilities and other barriers to employment to gain independence through the power of work."

Address: 4-21 27th Avenue, Astoria, NY 11102 (greater New York) and 400 Supor Boulevard, Harrison, NJ 07029 (northern New Jersey)

Telephone: 718-728-5400 (New York) and 973-474-2001 (New Jersey)

Website: http://www.goodwillnynj.org/

Department of Labor and Workforce Development (Division of Vocational Rehabilitation)

Mission: "Enable individuals with disabilities to achieve employment outcomes consistent with their strengths, priorities, needs, abilities, and capabilities."

Address: 990 Broad Street, 2nd Floor, Newark, NJ 07101

Telephone: 973-648-3494

Website:

http://lwd.dol.state.nj.us/labor/roles/disable/ and

http://jobs4jersey.com/jobs4jersey/jobseekers/disable/index.html

The New Jersey Division of the Deaf and Hard of Hearing

Mission: "The New Jersey Division of the Deaf and Hard of Hearing is the principal state agency established by New Jersey Law (PL 1977, C. 166) on behalf of people of all ages who are deaf and hard of hearing. The division provides education, advocacy, and direct services to eliminate barriers and promote increased accessibility to programs, services, and information routinely available to the state's general population."

Address: 990 Broad Street, 2nd Floor, Newark, NJ 07101

Telephone: 973-648-3494

Website:

http://www.state.nj.us/humanservices/ddh

h/home/index.html

The New Jersey Division of Mental Health

Services

Mission: "The mission of the New Jersey

Division of Mental Health Services is to

promote opportunities for adults with

serious mental illness to maximize their

abilities to live, work, socialize, and learn in

communities of their choice."

Address: 990 Broad Street, 2nd Floor,

Newark, NJ 07101

Telephone: 973-648-3494

Website:

http://www.state.nj.us/humanservices/dm

hs/home/index.html

National Organization on Disability (NOD)

Mission: "NOD is a private, nonprofit

organization that promotes the full

participation and contributions of America's

56 million people with disabilities in all

aspects of life. Today, the NOD focuses on

increasing employment opportunities for

the 79 percent of working-age Americans

with disabilities who are not employed."

Address: 77 Water Street, Suite 204,

New York, NY 10005

Telephone: 646-505-1191 ext. 122

Website: http://nod.org/

Office of Disability Employment Policy (ODEP)

Mission: "ODEP's mission is to develop and influence policies and practices that increase the number and quality of employment opportunities for people with disabilities."

Address: 200 Constitution Avenue, NW Washington DC, 20210

Telephone: 1-866-ODEP-DOL (633-7365)

Website: http://www.dol.gov/odep/about/

United Spinal Association

Mission: "United Spinal Association is dedicated to improving the quality of life for all Americans with spinal cord injuries and disorders."

Address: 75-20 Astoria Boulevard, Jackson Heights, NY 11370-1177

Telephone: 718-803-3782

Website: www.unitedspinal.org

Employment and Other Important Data

The Numbers Don't Lie

The following tables shows the population size and unemployment rates among individuals with disabilities in Ohio, New Jersey, New York, Washington DC, Maryland, and Georgia. The table below displays the population size from 1990 (the year the Americans with Disabilities Act was enacted) to today. This information includes the total population size during that time, the population size of those with disabilities, the total unemployment rate for each state, and the unemployment rate of individuals with disabilities in each state. The information compiled below

represents individuals between the ages of 16 to

64.

Ohio

Population and Unemployment Rate- Ohio				
Years	Population Size	Population Size of Those with a Disability	Ohio Unemployment Rate	Unemployment Rate of Those with a Disability
1990	6,860,534	304,383	6.0	32.7
2000	7,186,632	722,527	4.0	23.3
2008	11,310,700	1,481,300	6.6	10.6
2013	11,398,298	1,555,348	7.4	10.4

The information compiled above was created by
using the information from the United States
Census Bureau (www.census.gov), Bureau of Labor
Statistics (www.bls.gov), and Disability Statistics
(www.disabilitystatistics.org).

The Ohio data displays that between 1990 and 2000, the population size increased 326,098. In regards to individuals with a disability, the population size more than doubled from 304,383 to 722,527. What this possibly shows is that with the Americans with Disability Act (ADA) of 1990, people started to come forward in record numbers to disclose their disability with hopes of getting assistance with overcoming their disability and obtaining employment. The unemployment rate for Ohioans in 1990 with and without disabilities was unable to be found. This could be due to research about the population's unemployment rates not being available during this time because it was not being completed.

In looking at the data from 2000 to 2008, the population size increased 4,124,068. In regards to individuals with a disability, the population size again more than doubled from 722,527 to 1,445,054. The increase in individuals with disabilities could possibly be attributed to the amendments to ADA, known as the Americans with Disabilities Act Amendments (ADAA). The ratifications of this act took place in 2008 and were actually implemented in 2009. The unemployment rate for Ohioans in 2000 was 4.0. The unemployment rate for individuals with disabilities is not displayed. The information found was only for the years of 2008 to 2012. In 2008, the unemployment rate was 6.6 and 10.6% for those individuals with a disability. This information shows that individuals with a disability were at a disproportionate disadvantage of having a disability and being unemployed compared to individuals without a disability.

Reviewing data from 2008 to 2013 reveals that the population size only increased 87,598 within five years. In regards to individuals with a disability, the increase was only 74,048. This information displays that the rate of individuals reporting having a disability decreased somewhat, which could potentially mean that Ohio has done a great job of early detection of disabilities and possibly prevention of work related injuries. The unemployment rate for Ohioans in 2013 (actually 2012's numbers) was 7.4% and 10.4% for those individuals with a disability. The 2012 data was the only disability information available at this time in

researching this information.

New Jersey

Population and Unemployment Rate- New Jersey				
Years	Populat ion Size	Populat ion of Those with a Disabili ty	New Jersey Unempl oyment Rate	Unempl oyment Rate of Those with a Disabilit y
1990	5,030,2 93	239,54 8	5.8	28.1
2000	5,362,2 42	405,01 9	4.5	25.0
2008	8,571,6 00	841,50 0	5.5	8.2
2013	8,791,6 52	935,83 3	8.2	13.8

The information compiled above was created by
using the information from the United States
Census Bureau (www.census.gov), Bureau of Labor
Statistics (www.bls.gov), and Disability Statistics
(www.disabilitystatistics.org).

New Jersey data shows that between 1990 and 2000, the total population had increased 331,949. In regards to individuals with a disability, the increase was nearly double from 239,548 to 405,019. The disability increase was possibly also attributed to ADA of 1990. The unemployment rate for New Jersey in 1990 with and without disabilities was unable to be found. This could be due to research about the population's unemployment rates not being available during this time because it was not being completed.

In reviewing the data from 2000 to 2008, the total population increased 3,209,358. In regards to individuals with a disability, the increase was more than double from 405,019 to 841, 500. The disability increase was possibly also attributed to ratifications of ADAA of 2008 and implementation of 2009. The unemployment rate in 2000 was 4.5. The unemployment rate for individuals with disabilities is not displayed in the chart. In 2008, the unemployment rate for the total population was 5.5% and 8.2% for individuals with disabilities. This information shows that, similar to Ohio, individuals with disabilities in New Jersey were also at a disproportionate disadvantage of having a disability and being unemployed compared to individuals without a disability.

From 2008 to 2013, the total population size increased 220,052. In regards to individuals with a disability, the increase was only 94,333. The increase in disabilities could also be similar to Ohio where New Jersey is implementing early detection procedures and there are fewer work-related injuries. The unemployment rate in 2013 was 8.2% for the total New Jersey population and 13.8% for individuals with disabilities. Again, this shows that, similar to Ohio, individuals with disabilities in New Jersey were also at a disproportionate disadvantage of having a disability and being unemployed compared to individuals without a disability.

New York

Population and Unemployment Rate- New York				
Years	Population Size	Population of Those with a Disability	New York Unemployment Rate	Unemployment Rate of Those with a Disability
1990	11,655,889	664,346	5.8	34.4

2000	12,193,044	1,130,439	5.2	28.8
2008	19,239,200	2,155,500	5.4	7.5
2013	19,400,069	2,171,581	7.7	9.6

The information compiled above was created by using the information from the United States Census Bureau (www.census.gov), Bureau of Labor Statistics (www.bls.gov), and Disability Statistics (www.disabilitystatistics.org).

New York data shows that between 1990 and 2000, the population size increased 537,155. In regards to individuals with a disability, the total population nearly doubled from 664,346 to 1,130,439. This increase of those with disabilities could also be similar to Ohio and New Jersey, where the increase could potentially be due to ADA of 1990 and individuals with disabilities coming forth. The unemployment rate for 1990 for individuals with and without disabilities was unable to be found.

From 2000 to 2008, the data shows that the total population size increased 7,046,156. In regards to those with disabilities, the population nearly doubled from 1,130,439 to 2,155,500. The disability increase was also possibly attributed to ratifications of ADAA of 2008 and implementation of 2009. The unemployment rate in 2000 for the total population of New York was 5.2%. The unemployment rate for individuals with disabilities is also not displayed. In 2008, the unemployment rate was 5.4% for the total population and 7.5% for those individuals with disabilities. This information shows that similar to Ohio and New Jersey, individuals with disabilities in New York were also at a disproportionate disadvantage of having a disability and being unemployed compared to individuals without a disability.

The data from 2008 to 2013 displays that the total population size increased 160,869. In regards to those with a disability; the increase was only by 16,081 this time. The increase in disabilities could also be similar to Ohio and New Jersey where New York is implementing early detection procedures and there are fewer work-related injuries. The unemployment rate for the total population for New York in 2013 was 7.7 for the total population and 9.6% for those individuals with a disability. Again, this shows that similar to Ohio and New Jersey, individuals with disabilities in New York were also at a disproportionate disadvantage of having a disability and being unemployed compared to individuals without a disability.

Washington, DC

Population and Unemployment Rate- Washington DC				
Years	Population Size	Population of Those with a Disability	DC Unemployment Rate	Unemployment Rate of Those with a Disability
1990	411,385	29,124	6.6	33.8
2000	391,946	37,645	6.5	30.2
2008	583,900	63,700	6.6	10.2
2013	635,833	68,830	8.3	10.4

The information compiled above was created by using the information from the United States Census Bureau (www.census.gov), Bureau of Labor Statistics (www.bls.gov), and Disability Statistics (www.disabilitystatistics.org).

The data for Washington, DC displays that from 1990 to 2000, the total population size decreased 19,439. With this decrease, the number of individuals with a disability during that time still increased from 29,124 to 37,645. The increase of those with a disability could be similar to Ohio, New Jersey, and New York where the increase was possibly attributed to ADA of 1990. The unemployment rate for 1990 was also unable to be found for individuals with and without disabilities.

In reviewing the data from 2000 to 2008, the population size increased 191,954. In regards to those individuals with a disability; the size was nearly doubled from 37,645 to 63,700. The disability increase was also possibly attributed to ratifications of ADAA of 2008 and implementation of 2009. The unemployment rate for the total population of Washington, DC in 2000 was 6.5%. The unemployment rate for individuals with disabilities is not displayed in the chart. In 2008, the unemployment rate was 6.6% for the total population and 10.2% for those individuals with disabilities. This information displays that similar to Ohio, New Jersey, and New York, individuals with disabilities in Washington, DC were also at a disproportionate disadvantage of having a disability and being unemployed compared to individuals without a disability.

The data from 2008 to 2013 displays that the population size increased 51,933. In regards to those with a disability, the increase was only 5,130. The increase in disabilities could also be similar to

Ohio, New Jersey, and New York where

Washington, DC is implementing early detection

procedures and there are fewer work-related

injuries. The unemployment rate for the total

population was 8.3% and 10.4% for those

individuals with disabilities. Again, this displays that

similar to Ohio, New Jersey, and New York,

individuals with disabilities in Washington, DC were

also at a disproportionate disadvantage of having a

disability and being unemployed compared to

individuals without a disability.

Maryland

Population and Unemployment Rate- Maryland

Years	Population Size	Population of Those with a Disability	Maryland Unemployment Rate	Unemployment Rate of Those with a Disability
1990	3,137,484	145,624	5.7	23.8
2000	3,412,197	285,852	3.6	22.4
2008	5,563,100	567,300	4.3	9.2
2013	5,834,039	622,682	6.6	12.6

The information compiled above was created by using the information from the United States Census Bureau (www.census.gov), Bureau of Labor Statistics (www.bls.gov), and Disability Statistics (www.disabilitystatistics.org).

Maryland data displays that from 1990 to2000, the population size increased 274,713. In regards to individuals with disabilities, the population size nearly doubled from 145,624 to

285,852. The increase of those with a disability could be similar to Ohio, New Jersey, New York, and Washington, DC where the increase was possibly attributed to ADA of 1990. The unemployment rate for 1990 was also unable to be found for individuals with and without disabilities.

In reviewing the data from 2000 to 2008, the population size increased 2,150,903. In regards to individuals with disabilities, the population size nearly doubled from 285,852 to 567,300. The disability increase was also possibly attributed to ratifications of ADAA of 2008 and implementation of 2009. The unemployment rate for the total population for individuals in Maryland in 2000 was 3.6%. The unemployment rate for individuals with disabilities is not displayed in the chart. In 2008, the unemployment rate for the total population was 4.3% and for those with a disability was 9.2%. This information displays that similar to Ohio, New Jersey, New York, and Washington, DC individuals with disabilities in Maryland were also at a disproportionate disadvantage of having a disability and being unemployed compared to individuals without a disability. Individuals with a disability were more than two times as likely to be unemployed than those individuals who did not have a disability.

From 2008 to 2013, the population size increased from 270,939. In regards to people with disabilities, the increase was 55,382. The slight increase in those with a disability in comparison to the other years could also be similar to Ohio, New

Jersey, New York, and Washington DC where

Maryland is implementing early detection

procedures and there are fewer work-related

injuries. In 2013, the unemployment rate for the

total population was 6.6% and for those with a

disability was 12.6%. Again, this displays that

similar to Ohio, New Jersey, New York, and

Washington, DC., individuals with disabilities in

Maryland were also at a disproportionate

disadvantage of having a disability and being

unemployed compared to an individuals without a

disability.

Georgia

Population and Unemployment Rate- Georgia

Years	Population Size	Percentage of Those with a Disability	Georgia Unemployment Rate	Unemployment Rate of Those with a Disability
1990	4,161,119	220,744	5.2	28.7
2000	5,306,618	507,990	3.8	25.1
2008	9,537,200	1,115,500	6.3	9.9
2013	9,800,887	1,211,831	8.2	11.1

The information compiled above was created by using the information from the United States Census Bureau (www.census.gov), Bureau of Labor Statistics (www.bls.gov), and Disability Statistics (www.disabilitystatistics.org).

Georgia data displays that from 1990 to 2000, the total population size increased 1,145,499. In regards to individuals with a disability, the increase was more than double from

220,744 to 507,990. The increased population size of those with a disability could be similar to Ohio, New Jersey, New York, Washington, DC and Maryland where the increase was possibly attributed to ADA of 1990. The unemployment rate for 1990 was also unable to be found for individuals with and without disabilities.

From 2000 to 2008, the population increased 4,230,582. In regards to individuals with disabilities, the increase more than doubled going from 507,990 to 1,115,500. The disability increase was also possibly attributed to ratifications of ADAA of 2008 and implementation of 2009. The unemployment rate for the total population in Georgia for 2000 was 3.8%. The unemployment rate for individuals with disabilities was is not displayed in the chart. In 2008, the unemployment rate for the total population was 6.3% and 9.9% for individuals with disabilities. This information displays that similar to Ohio, New Jersey, New York, Washington, DC, and Maryland, individuals with disabilities in Georgia were also at a disproportionate disadvantage of having a disability and being unemployed compared to individuals without a disability.

In reviewing the data from 2008 to 2013, the population increased 263,687. In regards to individuals with a disability, the increase was 96,331. The slight increase in those with a disability in comparison to the other years could also be similar to Ohio, New Jersey, New York, Washington DC, and Maryland where Georgia is implementing

early detection procedures and there are fewer
work-related injuries. In 2013, the unemployment
rate for the total population was 8.2% and 11.1%
for those individuals with a disability. Again, this
displays that similar to Ohio, New Jersey, New
York, Washington, DC, and Maryland, individuals
with disabilities in Georgia were also at a
disproportionate disadvantage of having a
disability and being unemployed compared to
individuals without a disability.

What the data above goes to show and
what can be assumed is that individuals with
disabilities make up less than 10% of the United
States population, but their unemployment
accounts for, at the most, 13% of the
unemployment rates. Disabled individuals are at a

disproportionate disadvantage because they make up less than half of the U.S. population but have a higher unemployment rate than the general population. In looking at unemployment rates, I chose to look at individuals between the ages of 16 to 64 and those who were without a job, but actively searching. This eliminated the number of individuals who were under the working age and those who were not actually seeking employment.

Work Opportunity Tax Credit

Some employers may not be aware that they may receive tax breaks for hiring individuals with a documented disability or other selected targeted populations. The Work Opportunity Tax Credit (WOTC) is "a Federal tax credit available to employers for hiring individuals from certain target groups who have consistently faced significant barriers to employment" (United Stated Department of Labor, 2014). The employer hiring these individuals will have to complete an IRS Form 8850 and either an ETA Form 9061 or ETA Form 9062. Once these forms have been completed, the employer has 28 days to submit the forms to the state's Department of Labor and Workforce Development. What this means is that certain disability information would have to be disclosed by the employer in order for the company to obtain the tax credit.

The table below shows the credit amounts employers could potentially get.

WOTC Target Groups	
Short-Term TANF Recipient	$2400
Long-Term TANF Recipient	$9000 (Over 2 years)
SNAP (Food stamp) Recipient	$2400
Designated Community Resident	$2400
Vocational Rehabilitation Referral	$2400
Ex-Felon	$2400
SSI Recipient	$2400
Summer Youth	$1200

The information compiled above was created by using the information from the United States Department of Labor (http://www.doleta.gov/business/incentives/opptax/benefits.cfm

The table above displays that individuals with a disability could potentially fit within any category listed and even veteran target group population. The veteran target group population information is not listed in this text due to the information reflecting that individuals qualify for tax credits due to their veteran status and not their disability status. Many service providers are aware that although the veteran information does not list disability specific information, there's a possibility that individuals could still fall under this category. This is the reason it is suggested that a thorough evaluation be completed on the Department of Labor's website, which is listed underneath the table above. If employers want more information and assistance in understanding how to access these credits, it would be in an employer's best interest to speak with a representative from the Department of Labor within their state. The representative would be able to answer the employer's questions about the required documents that have to be submitted within 28 days.

Job developers and preplacement employees generally use the WOTC as a way to assist companies with hiring an individual with a disability. The WOTC provides employers with additional resources that allows companies to make necessary workplace modifications and give individuals well deserved opportunities. There are definitely individuals who have a disability who really want to work. I have been in contact with these individuals on numerous occasions who work hard by attending work readiness class, attend training every day, partake in testing, and learn various skills to be job ready. Of course, not every skill can be taught to ever individual. For example, autistic individuals may always struggle with social skills. In these situations, developers work toward educating the employer about working with individuals who may lack certain social skills. Developers are unable to disclose disability information unless the consumer has signed a consent for release form that gives the person an ability to disclose the information. In thinking about the work opportunity take form, the consumer must recognize that in order for the employer to obtain a tax credit, disability information would have to be disclosed.

2015 Employment Challenge

Whether you are an employer, service provider, or part of a support system, I challenge you to think outside the box to see how we can help people with disabilities. Thinking outside the box involves having an open mind, doing all that needs to be done to make this population successful, and being an advocate. Sometimes providers within the field and family members can be closed minded in regards to what an individual can do. We sometimes have to allow others to see the positive in individuals with disabilities and accentuate their positive traits and ways to make them successful.

Within the past eight years that I have been working with this population, I have witnessed people stating that an individual could not do a particular activity or was not skilled enough to do it. With the right training, patience, and diligence from a service provider this individual was able to accomplish what most people deemed impossible. What this shows is that individuals can learn a skill and master it. Sometimes it takes them a longer time to master the skills, but it is a well-known fact that individuals with disabilities tend to stay with companies for many years. There is not a high turnover rate for individuals who have disabilities, and a lot of companies retain skilled employees.

So I leave you here today challenging you to think outside the box and develop creative ways to help those with disabilities obtain and maintain employment. Helping people is good for the soul and it makes you feel good.

Famous People with Disabilities

50 Tyson- Rapper/song writer (autism)

Muhammad Ali- Boxer (Parkinson's disease)

Alexander Graham Bell- Inventor of the

telephone (dyslexia)

Jim Carey- Actor/comedian (ADHD)

Cher- Singer (dyslexia)

Tom Cruise- Actor (dyslexia)

Charles Darwin- Naturalist/author (OCD)

Cameron Diaz- Actress (OCD)

Walt Disney- Owner of Walt Disney World

(learning disability)

Albert Einstein- Mathematician/physicist

(autism/learning disability)

Geri Jewell- Comedian/actress (cerebral palsy)

Helen Keller- Author/activist/lecturer. (Deaf/blind)

Jenifer Lewis- Actress/comedian/singer (bipolar)

Richard Pryor- Comedian/actor/writer (multiple sclerosis)

Franklin Delano Roosevelt- President (polio)

Donald Sutherland- Actor (polio)

Ludwig van Beethoven- Composer/musician (deaf)

Damon Wayans- Comedian/actor (club feet)

Robin Williams- Actor/comedian (ADHD)

Stevie Wonder- Musician/singer/songwriter

(blind)

Commonly Used Words and/or Acronyms

ADHD- Attention Deficit Hyper Activity Disorder

BSP- Behavior Support Plan

BA- Benefits Analysis

CBA- Community Based Assessment

CD- Cognitive Disorder

Competitive Employment

Consumers

Creative housing

Customers

Day Services

DD- Developmental Disabilities

ED- Emotional Disorder

Group home

ID- Intellectual Disability

IEP- Individual Education Plan

IPE- Individual Plan of Employment

Integration

Institutionalized

ISP- Individual Service Plan

Job Coaching

Job Development

Job Retention

LD- Learning Disability

OCD- Obsessive Compulsive Disorder

OOD- Opportunities for Ohioans with Disabilities Participants

PASS- Plan for Achieving Self Sufficiency

Rehab Staff – Vocational Rehabilitation Staff

RSC- Rehabilitation Services Commission

SLD- Specific Learning Disability

SLE- Structured Learning Experience

Sheltered

Employment

Supported

Employment

TBI- Traumatic Brain

Injury

Trial Work Period

VR- Vocational

Rehabilitation

Services

Vocational Evaluation

WAT- Work

Adjustment Training

WR- Work Readiness

Revealing Something About the Author

Melica Niccole has found it very easy to relate to individuals with disabilities and accept them as integral members of society. As a child, Melica struggled with becoming integrated into society through the activity of socialization. In fact, many of Melica's extended family members thought she was a mute because she did not socialize much with them. Socializing with others has always been a process for Melica. She ultimately knows that socialization is needed, to sustain a connectedness with others. She was not diagnosed with having any type of disability as a child; however, she uses empathy with individuals with disabilities due to her previous experience.

Currently, Melica works for a well-known non-profit agency where she trains and develops the social and work skills of individuals with various disabilities for competitive employment purposes. She has ten years in the human services field and over eight years of experience in the field doing job development, job coaching, community- based assessments, individual and group work adjustment, and supervising rehabilitation programs. Melica enjoys seeing the success of others in areas that were once thought impossible. Melica believes that it is not impossible; the possibilities lie in those ready to make a way. So make a way today by assisting those who may have

various challenges with obtaining paid

employment.

Work Cited

Black Entertainment Television (BET). Jenifer Lewis
Opens Up About Battle With Bipolar
Disorder. Retrieved from
http://www.bet.com/news/lifestyle/2014/0
1/28/jenifer-lewis-opens-up-about-battle-
with-bipolar-disorder.html
Accessed on 12/14/14

Brain Injury Alliance New Jersey. The Brain Injury
Association of American (BIAA) had
developed the following definitions, 2014.
Retrieved from http://bianj.org/about-
brain-injury.
Accessed on 12/19/14

Bureau of Labor Statistics- Local Area
Unemployment Statistics 1990. Retrieved
from
http://data.bls.gov/map/MapToolServlet?s
urvey=la&map=state&seasonal=u
Accessed on 12/7/14

Bureau of Labor Statistics- Local Area
Unemployment Statistics 2000. Retrieved
from http://www.bls.gov/lau/lastch00.htm

Accessed on 12/7/14

Bureau of Labor Statistics- Local Area
Unemployment Statistics 2008. Retrieved
from http://www.bls.gov/lau/lastch08.htm
Accessed on 12/7/14

Bureau of Labor Statistics- Local Area
Unemployment Statistics 2013. Retrieved
from http://www.bls.gov/lau/lastch13.htm
Accessed on 12/7/14

Centers for Disease Control and Prevention. Autism
Spectrum Disorder (ASD), 2014. Retrieved
from
http://www.cdc.gov/ncbddd/autism/index.
html.
Accessed on 12/19/14

Centers for Disease Control and Prevention.
Attention-Deficit/Hyperactivity Disorder
(ADHD), 2014. Retrieved from
http://www.cdc.gov/ncbddd/adhd/index.ht
ml.
Accessed on 12/19/14

Centers for Disease Control and Prevention.
Cerebral Palsy (CP), 2014. Retrieved from
http://www.cdc.gov/ncbddd/cp/index.html
Accessed on 12/19/14

Centers for Disease Control and Prevention. Data
and Statistics, 2014. Retrieved from
http://www.cdc.gov/ncbddd/birthdefects/d
ata.html
Accessed on 12/7/14

Centers for Disease Control and Prevention.
Developmental Disabilities; 2013. Retrieved
from
http://www.cdc.gov/ncbddd/developmenta
ldisabilities/index.html
Accessed on 12/19/14

Centers for Disease Control and Prevention. Facts
about Intellectual Disability. Retrieved from
http://www.cdc.gov/ncbddd/actearly/pdf/p
arents_pdfs/IntellectualDisability.pdf
Accessed on 12/19/14

Centers for Disease Control and Prevention. Facts
about Vision Loss. Retrieved from
http://www.cdc.gov/ncbddd/actearly/pdf/p
arents_pdfs/VisionLossFactSheet.pdf
Accessed on 12/19/14

Centers for Disease Control and Prevention. Fragile
X syndrome (FXS), 2014. Retrieved from
http://www.cdc.gov/ncbddd/fxs/index.html
.
Accessed on 12/19/14

Channel 4. Prototype. Retrieved from
https://www.youtube.com/watch?v=jA8in
mHhx8c
Accessed on 12/19/14

Disability Statistics. 2000 Disability Status Report.
Retrieved from
http://www.disabilitystatistics.org/reports/
census.cfm?statistic=1
Accessed on 12/20/14

Disability Statistics. 2008 Disability Status Report.
Retrieved from
http://www.disabilitystatistics.org/StatusRe
ports/2008-PDF/2008-StatusReport_OH.pdf
Accessed on 12/7/14

Disability Statistics. 2008 Disability Status Report.
Retrieved from
http://www.disabilitystatistics.org/reports/
acs.cfm?statistic=1
Accessed on 12/20/14

Disability Statistics. Not Working but Actively
Looking for Work; 2008. Retrieved from
http://www.disabilitystatistics.org/reports/
acs.cfm?statistic=3
Accessed on 12/17/14

Disability Statistics. Not Working but Actively
Looking for Work; 2012. Retrieved from
http://www.disabilitystatistics.org/reports/
acs.cfm?statistic=3
Accessed on 12/20/14

Disabled World. Famous People with Disabilities.
http://www.disabled-
world.com/artman/publish/article_0060.sht
ml
Accessed on 12/17/14

Gallaudet University. Emotional/Behavioral
Disorders. Retrieved from
http://www.gallaudet.edu/clerc_center/inf
ormation_and_resources/info_to_go/educa
te_children_%283_to_21%29/students_wit
h_disabilities/emotionalbehavioral_disorde
rs.html
Accessed on 12/19/14

Huffington Post. 10 Majorly Successful People with
Disabilities. Retrieved from
http://www.huffingtonpost.com/2013/10/2
2/famous-people-with-
disabilities_n_4142930.html
Accessed on 12/19/14

Hill Country Disabled Group. The World's Most
Famous Disabled People
Retrieved from http://hcdg.org/famous.htm

Accessed on 12/14/14

Kim-Rupnow, W., Ph.D; (2001). An Introduction to
        Korean Culture for Rehabilitation Service
        Providers; Attitudes toward Disability.
        Retrieved from
        http://cirrie.buffalo.edu/culture/monograp
        hs/korea/#s4b
        Accessed on 12/7/14

King, Jr., M. I Have a Dream; 1963. Retrieved from
        http://www.americanrhetoric.com/speeche
        s/mlkihaveadream.htm
        Accessed on 12/19/14

Learning RX. Specific Learning Disabilities-
Definitions 2014. Retrieved from
        http://www.learningrx.com/specific-
learning-disabilities.htm
        Accessed on 12/19/14

Learning RX. Cognitive Disorders; 2014. Retrieved
        from
        http://www.learningrx.com/cognitive-
        disorders-faq.htm
        Accessed on 12/19/14

National Institutes of Health. National Institutes of
        Neurological Disorders and Stroke. Tourette
        Syndrome Fact Sheet. Retrieved from

http://www.ninds.nih.gov/disorders/touret
te/detail_tourette.htm

National Institutes of Health; Medline Plus. Down
syndrome. Retrieved from
http://vsearch.nlm.nih.gov/vivisimo/cgi-
bin/query-
meta?v%3Aproject=medlineplus&query=do
wn+syndrome&x=13&y=11)
Accessed on 12/19/14

National Institutes of Health; Medline Plus.
Seizures, 2014. Retrieved from
http://www.nlm.nih.gov/medlineplus/ency/
article/003200.htm
Accessed on 12/19/14
Ohio Department of Developmental Disabilities.
Definitions. Retrieved from
https://doddportal.dodd.ohio.gov/glossary/
Pages/default.aspx
Accessed on 12/19/14

Rain Man. Dir. Barry Levinson. Metro-Goldwyn-
Mayer Studios Inc, 1988. Film

Roosevelt Institute. Polio Strikes. Retrieved from
http://rooseveltinstitute.org/policy-and-
ideasroosevelt-historyfdr/polio-strikes
Accessed on 12/14/14

Taking the MR out of MRDD. Retrieved from

https://www.youtube.com/watch?v=VVCgJ
TcalRY
Accessed on 12/14/14

TeachHub.com. 12 Successful Stars with Learning
Disabilities. Retrieved From
http://www.teachhub.com/12-successful-
stars-learning-disabilities
Accessed on 12/20/14

Unforgotten: Twenty-Five Years after Willowbrook.
Documentary. FilmRise, 2014. YouTube
https://www.youtube.com/watch?v=FcjRIZ
FQcUY
Accessed on 12/20/14

United States Census Bureau. American Fact
Finder. 2000 Unemployment 21-64 Years of
Age. Retried from
http://factfinder.census.gov/faces/tableser
vices/jsf/pages/productview.xhtml?pid=DE
C_00_110S_PCT032&prodType=table
Accessed on 2/23/15

United States Census Bureau. Disability
Characteristics 1990 Census. Retrieved from
https://www.census.gov/people/disability/
methodology/census.html
Accessed on 2/23/15

United States Census Bureau. Disability Characteristics. 2013 American Community Survey 1-Year Estimates. Retrieved from file:///C:/Users/Melica/Downloads/2013dis ability.pdf
Accessed on 12/20/14

United States Census Bureau. Disability among the Working Age Population: 2008 and 2009. Retrieved from http://www.census.gov/prod/2010pubs/acs br09-12.pdf
Accessed on 12/7/14

United States Census Bureau. Nearly 1 in 5 People Have a Disability in the U.S., Census Bureau Reports. https://www.census.gov/newsroom/releas es/archives/miscellaneous/cb12-134.html
Accessed on 12/20/14

United States Census Bureau. With a work disability (WD), a mobility limitation (ML) or a self-care limitation (SCL) Retrieved from http://www.census.gov/people/disability/m ethodology/census/tables/tab1st.txt
Accessed on 12/20/14

United States Department of Labor. Employment and Training Administration. Retrieved from

http://www.doleta.gov/business/incentives/opptax/benefits.cfm
Accessed on 12/20/14